Diary of a Schizophrenic

Bethany Boik

For information about this title or to order other books and/or electronic media, contact the publisher:
Two Sisters Writing & Publishing®
TwoSistersWriting.com
18530 Mack Avenue, Suite 166
Grosse Pointe Farms, MI 48236

ISBN 978-1-956879-42-1 (Paperback)
ISBN 978-1-956879-38-4 (eBook)

Printed in the United States of America

All the stories in this work are true.
Cover Design: Michael Lancaster.
Cover Creation and Graphic Design: Illumination Graphics.
Paintings by Bethany Boik.

DEDICATION & ACKNOWLEDGMENTS

This book is dedicated to everyone living with a mental illness who gets up every day and lives life despite all the pain they experience each waking second.

This book is also for my tenth-grade English teacher Mr. D, who encouraged me to dream big and never give up. As well as Ryan and Brett, two of my "found family" members, who without you two, I might not be writing these words. Thank you all for cheering me on as well as saving my life in countless ways. I love you all.

I would also like to thank the rest of my found family: Ruth, Adrienne, Navneet and Rachel. And Mike, a friend who took my cover photos for this book. Thank you for taking the time to listen.

As well as the love of my life Jer, you make me smile more than any amount of glitter and unicorns surrounding me. And that's a big deal. Thank you, Jer, for showing me what relentless support really means. I love you with my entire being.

I would also like to thank the woman who made me who I am today: my grandma. I thank you for giving me my caring spirit. You forever changed the course of my life. And I couldn't forget to mention my Godfather Kevin; with your continued lifelong love and support, I feel incredibly loved.

Thank you, everyone!

CONTENTS

FOREWORD

by Ryan Carrow

"I am fighting my losses, trauma, and everything bringing ache because I don't want to look in the mirror and see a tragedy staring back."

—Noor Unnahar

Bethany had a four-foot-tall tree branch that was cemented into an ornately decorated pot. She had painted the various appendages of the branch with a multitude of colorful paints. To the tree, a rainbow of feathers and puff balls was adhered. It was described as her Happy Tree. This tree was more representative of the Bethany I had come to know. When I first met her, she had decorated her room with artwork much like this tree. The artwork later became apparent to be an outward representation of herself. Bethany is a colorful person, but like most of her pieces, she also could be fragile.

We met during our time in college. We would gather in the student lounge and were introduced through mutual friends. We had decided to hang out and I invited her over to my home. She seemed to enjoy just chatting and being around me. Bethany got really excited by one thing in my home: my cheese drawer! She made countless quesadillas and never seemed to get tired of them.

One evening, Bethany mentioned how she was able to sleep well at our house. This eventually led to her becoming my roommate. Her room was vibrantly painted in Apricot Flower (a pale orange). She never changed the color and later added black curtains. She decorated her room with artwork that she created, quotes upon quotes, and her books. She had 10 mattress-toppers and looked like she was the princess and the pea.

Before I knew her, I realized I had never met anyone like her. Her art warned me of her dark side, but most artists I knew were troubled in some aspect of their life. Frankly, I didn't care about her problems if she was a compassionate and kind person.

Throughout the end of our college experience and her cyclical mental health experiences, we made countless memories together. We spent time laughing and crying. Sometimes I was her friend and sometimes I was something different. My husband and I would support her where we could, driving her to the hospital or helping her keep track of her medicine. We fought like siblings at times, but knew we would always reconcile.

Bethany had a vast number of wins and setbacks over this time. The only thing that was truly consistent was her perpetual motion forward. When she was knocked down and unable to walk, she would start her crawl forward—relentless, determined to tell her story and shine light on our struggling mental health system to reduce stigma by giving a face to her disease.

While I know some of her stories, it was impossible for her to tell me everything. Every time she got quiet in the car, she could be tired, but she may be having an audio or visual hallucination. She had exhausted the available prescriptions on many occasions and would be stuck with the residual effects of her undertreated disease. There were periods in our friendship where she was not safe to leave alone. She would sit in my nursing classes, or she would sit in the lobby of my job (within my view) while I worked. The paramount effect of health would overwhelm most people. Bethany has continued to show resilience and found passion in spreading awareness.

My husband, Brett, used to push her to finish the book and joke that she needed to think of us when she was published and sitting on Oprah's couch. When Bethany was ready to take the next steps in her life, it was a bittersweet time. Her symptoms were greatly controlled, and she had been able to secure an apartment. It felt like a great place for her to take this step. Since moving out, much like us, our relationship has continued to evolve and mature. I look back at the portion of our youth with fond memories. I find myself so elated at the fact that she has completed her book.

I love you, Beth; I am so proud of you!

POEM

I'm not a schizophrenic, so please don't call me one.

I'm a person who lives with schizophrenia.

A person who is accustomed to living with an invisible disease that no one sees

Till I'm out there falling on my knees.

It's hard when your brain is cracked to pieces and all your thoughts are swirling around.

No one sees you struggling till it's too late and your brain is scrambled half to death.

I'm trying to give you a picture of

A hell on earth diagnosis,

A cracked damaged brain,

Looking to kill me like a shark in the ocean eating its prey.

Yes, I pray to God, who talks to me on occasion.

Like the man on the street corner, I just want solitude.

The only difference between me and the guy on the corner of the block who talks to himself

Is I have access to medication, a shelter and I take all seven of my psychotropic medications on the daily.

If I didn't, I'd be dead. With nothing left to bother me in my head.

But that's where my thoughts get gritty.

And my illness sinks its teeth in.

It wants me to give in.

It haunts me, and paralyzes me with fear.

Some days I can't leave the house 'cause it feels like people are watching me and I can't leave my own room. Under my covers is the only place I feel safe. Sleep is the only rest I get. I feel anxious every minute I'm awake. I'm ready to explode from the inside out. The pressure is so bad and my chest tightens for days and days. I can't breathe properly.

I suffocate with fear. What do I do when the monsters are nearby?

I'm not a schizophrenic, so please don't call me one. I am a person who lives with schizophrenia—first and foremost—so get that right before you say it wrong.

I'm a human being with feelings, so please don't take this poem wrong.

The word schizophrenic has a negative connotation associated with it. I named this book Diary of a Schizophrenic *to capture people's attention. I am a person living with a form of schizophrenia—I am not a schizophrenic.*

INTRODUCTION

Diary of a Schizophrenic

My name is Bethany and you are holding my diary. I decided I wanted to decrease the stigma surrounding schizophrenia and schizoaffective disorder by baring it all in releasing my most vulnerable moments as a human.

This is the story of me growing up, starting at age 13 to age 31, with severe mental illness. This is my way of showing you what it's like to walk throughout my life with an illness that has, at times, broken my spirit, but never broke me. By sharing my story with you, I hope you get a better understanding of what it's like to be seriously mentally ill and live life in a neurotypical world.

On this day, I just want to be happy and undisturbed from my illness. Now it's your chance to read the pages that helped me through my greatest suffering—and into my ultimate chance at changing people's perspective. So, it's your chance to read my diary . . . will you do it?

You know my name and now you know I live with a form of schizophrenia called schizoaffective disorder. It's a brain disease that affects most everything I do. Everything except love and care for my family and the love of my life. I have no idea where I'd be without him or my additional "found family." I love them all to pieces.

This book is a mental health diary I started putting together when I was 13 years old. That's when I became mentally ill and started a journal, which I would use on occasion for the next 15 years. As the years went by, I captured a lot of powerful, sad and overwhelming moments. Heartbreaking episodes appeared again and again, but I realized I always came back up swinging. This journey not only shows you my story, but my art that I did during therapy and pictures at various stages to bring you as close to my life as possible. What is it really like to walk in my shoes as a person living with a form of schizophrenia?

PART 1

The Beginning
of
The Symptoms

WE'RE IN TROUBLE PAINTING

LETTER FROM MY GHOST

Let me remind you, my 13-year-old self was killed the day that the depression decided to wrap its heavy arms around my body, crushing my soul and my physical being. I became unable to move. This beast then put a curse on my lips to stop me from preaching to the God/s. When all I wanted was for someone, or something, to come and save me. All I got was a ghost of who I used to be following my pitiful being, crying, wailing into her hands, asking, "Why in the world did you kill her?"

Let me tell you. I no longer can produce prayers. **If there was or is a God, why did He think it would be OK to trap people in a body that yearns for death so frequently that they stop living?** Why would it be OK for me to start planning my own demise? Why the fuck would He let this happen?

I am 13 years old. I'm 13 years old.

Did you not know that my friends—true Happiness and Hope—were severed by my mind and all that remain are my eyes? I can see everyone around me so clearly, but they can't see me. This ghost is all I have left and she hates the person who resides in her body.

Mirror Image

I have a beautiful painted face to those who can see. My clothes are mostly full of color, though all I can see is black. No one knows what I see when I look in a mirror.

A horrible image then appears.

I look happy when I smile, but inside I'm full of denial.

I'm filled with anger and rage, though to onlookers, I seem tranquil and kind. I can fall to pieces at any time. My soul is crushed and full of fear. As I try to pick up the pieces, I don't know what to think. I can't ease the past or make the present better. For I can't be that perfect person I will never see looking right before me.

Seeing the Psychiatrist

I'm 13 years old and I'm seeing a psychiatrist for the first time. I am nervous as I sit in the waiting room. I think, *What if they can't find anything wrong with me?*

I don't understand what is going on in my head or my body right now. I sit quietly as I chew on my nails. When I finally see the doctor, I tell her I can no longer sleep at night. Thoughts race in my head and I'm consumed by overwhelming anxiety and sadness. I'm afraid to call it melancholy, but I know it's worse than sadness. I just don't want to admit it at this time.

I'm scared and need help more than anything. I can't continue living this way. It's not OK.

The doctor tells me I have major depression, insomnia and an anxiety disorder. I am put on three medications.

ABILIFY

I'm 13.

My doctor puts me on a new medication. It's supposed to help with the psychosis.

I take one pill and I can't urinate for 48 hours; my pulse races. I'm in extreme pain. It feels like my bladder is going to explode.

I go to the hospital.

They tell me they don't have the equipment to help me, as I wasn't at a children's hospital.

They send me to Children's Hospital of Michigan.

They think I overdosed.

The doctors are mean to me and repeatedly ask me if I tried to kill myself; I say no.

"Are you bipolar?" they ask.

"No, I have depression—that's what my doctor said."

They say, "The medication you were put on was for something else."

It takes seven days for them to figure out what is wrong with me.

It was that one pill.

They say I had a severe allergic reaction to it.

My kidneys almost shut down.

High School, Part One

I go to my classes, now on four different medications—with one being an antipsychotic—all running through my veins. I try to function the best I can, but there are times where I can only manage to keep my head up for a few minutes and then I fall asleep and drool on myself and the desk. Clearly, I am a mess.

No one knows what is going on in my head. My school desk is just another bed. Some of my teachers think I'm a flunky. I failed my math class after my teacher refused to help me. She had no patience for the sad, sick goth kid who needed attention, and left me with an E.

I'm a good kid, I swear; I'm in marching band and drama club. I'm trying desperately to blend in and make friends. I want to have a good time in high school, but this is where the depressing shit begins. My mental illnesses are taking hold of me and I don't even understand the severity. My chest hurts, as if large fists had pounded me, over and over.

I'm tired.

I feel that I will fall to the ground if I stand any longer.

I sit down, but the room around me is still spinning.

I feel as if I have no air left to breathe.

The adrenaline inside is telling me to run, not just away from everyone, but to crawl out of my own skin.

I know that this will only last for 10 to 15 minutes, but every second feels like hours.

I sit in a classroom where almost 60 pairs of eyes are staring at me.

I am breathing heavily. I am hyperventilating now—I see a wheelchair coming down the row for me, pushed by the guidance office assistant.

I sit in the wheelchair mumbling to myself, not sure what to say.

I am so embarrassed and scared right now; the class is silent.

I am taken to the guidance office, where my grandma is called.

I just had a panic attack.

I see her.

As she locks eyes with me.

She reaches her arm out to pull me closer.

"I'm here to save you," she says.

"Save me?"

"Yes, save you."

"Save me from what?" I stammer.

"Save you from any and all hurt, pain, rejection and mental abuse. Just think about me and I'll pull you through."

I don't believe in much. But I believe her.

Lately it's been hard to brush my teeth and shower. And I'm in some kind of pain almost all the time. I want to scream daily for my higher power to take my physical and mental ailments away. That's if it's a day I actually believe in one.

You see, I'm sick of hearing voices tell me I'm worthless when my depression does the same damn thing.

So, I have to be saved, because something tells me that my life is worth more than being another suicide statistic. I am still going.

After I tried to kill myself, I'm still breathing and thinking and moving forward. There's got to be a damn good reason.

Therapy has been hit or miss. If you aren't jiving with a therapist, you need to find or ask for another one.

There will be one out there to help. You just have to

listen . . . listen with an objective ear. Because sometimes it's hard to hear things that *we* need to hear. We cover our ears and say we don't need to talk to someone. We stigmatize ourselves, say we are crazy. Or that only crazy people see psychiatrists or counselors.

But, you are not crazy, and getting a counselor is one of the best things you can do for yourself. You can save your life by taking a single step.

The Cuts That Didn't Heal

After having some school issues and a friend telling on me for cutting myself, I end up in "group." Group is a mixture of girls with problems.

Everything from being sexually abused to living with a drug addict to having bulimia, these girls have seen it all. The voices in my head argue: "Should you really be there?"

So, I mention that I tried cutting myself. My best friend at the time did it and she said it helped her cope with her problems. I saw the scars all the way down her wrists. I knew I shouldn't do it, but she said it helped.

So after she tells me this, I go home from school; I'm a little excited. *I'm going to try this,* I think. I hop into the shower with a grin on my face. I grab the razor and crack the blade off. I get even more excited. *What if it works?*

What if all my problems go away?

I don't want anyone to see the cuts, so I go for my inner thigh. I begin to cut. I do it fast and watch the blood run down the drain.

It's not working. I'm still hearing voices. I still feel numb. I take the razor again and again and cut myself until I have three lines of blood dripping down my leg. I fall over into the shower and begin to cry—not because I was in pain, but because *it didn't work.*

I never cut myself again.

As I lay here thinking about what has happened, looking into the future and the dark tomorrow, I can't help but to cry. My once beautiful, comfortable blanket turns to judgments and hate as it rapidly devours me and sews itself shut. The distinct but defined mark of depression floods over me, pulling me under. My anxiety and fears have buried me now. I no longer know who I am.

I don't remember when I saw myself last. It's been years since I have seen the real Bethany. I almost think a clear-headed, happy Bethany never existed. But I pray to God that she did, and that one day I will find her again.

I never wanted to cut myself until I thought it could help me. I thought it might take the pain of the voices and or paranoia and depression away. When it didn't work,

I became angry and more depressed than before. I was confused: why did this work for my friend and others, but not me? I knew cutting was a bad coping mechanism and told my friend what happened and told her to stop. She told me she was going for help. But then she told on me for what I did.

Cutting is not the answer. I promise you. All forms of body pain infliction do not have to occur. There are so many other ways to cope in a healthy way: exercise, like walking; listening to music; reading; writing poetry; screaming into a pillow; drawing; chewing gum; blowing bubbles and cooking.

It's hard to break a habit. I never caught on to cutting, but I've known people who have and have been free from it for a few years. Some of them quit and just said they are never going back; for others, it's more complex. They struggle every day. In the end, it's about support. And how to give yourself support through your journey.

That requires telling yourself how important you are and how worthy you are. Because at the finish line, it's all you in your glory!!! You are a shining star. I don't care what anyone else has ever said to you!! You are going to make it and I'm so proud!!!

High School, Part Two

I moved in eleventh grade. The new school I went to offered more advanced placement classes than the old one, and I was now able to take more English and Art classes. The move was difficult for me because I had only made acquaintances and not really close friends. But I was able to study and do homework after school with ease, because I didn't join clubs or have friendships. I did get bullied a lot, however.

I ate lunch in the bathroom a few times, so I didn't have to face the cafeteria, and I ran home from the bus stop because of guys harassing me and sometimes chasing me. I hated this school due to the bullying. But I never spoke up about it. So, nothing could have changed, so I don't blame them. They gave me a great education. I was just too scared to say anything.

My mental health was still in the forefront. I was on newer medication. I had tried more than eight medications by now and was realizing that medication management was difficult. And so was finding the right combination of medications for me.

Bethany

Age of Onset: 13

Misdiagnosed: Six years

New Diagnosis: Bipolar Disorder

An Enemy Within

"It might sound crazy," I think, "but at the end of this, I just want to survive."

"Why would you say that?" I ask myself.

Then I answer: "Because sometimes it feels like I'm at war with myself."

I feel like a prisoner trapped within my own skin. My mind is my captor and I'm at the mercy of my thoughts as they spin around me, suffocating my being.

I'm screaming and no one hears. I'm crying and they can only see the tears. The pain is so much more than the tiny droplets of water on my face.

I want this to stop. I'm sick of being in my head. It's like living in my own tortured hell as I attempt to come back to the surface.

Thoughts are quick. Thoughts are fast. Thoughts are racing. Thoughts are gone.

Numb, numb, numb, another episode done. I'm still alive. I can live. I can breathe. I can do anything.

I remind myself that I can and will survive—I will not **give** up. I will win this war, this battle within my mind.

PART II

Tell Them
My Story

TELL THEM MY STORY

With a chronic mental illness, Recovery is a fable.

As seen when "normal" functioning is temporary, and episodes reappear.

Thus, you are instead indebted, as a **prisoner**, trapped—

At the mercy of your mind—You can fall to pieces at any time.

Life is taken from you, **stolen** in increments.

Your rationality is fogged, overturned by **paranoia** and you ask how—

How do you move?

How do you continue to go, if you know it'll eventually sneak back?

The answer: you fight, that's what you do. You fight!

You realize what you're up against and you fight for survival.

So, I ask of you, to *please* not say those words of falsehood, but instead say what I really am.

Say what I'm really doing. Tell them I am a fighter.

Ghost Story, Part One

There's a ghost that follows me everywhere I go. It sits on my lap when I need rest. Never gives me a moment to breathe. Puts Its arms around my neck and tries to cry into my body.

It doesn't let me go. I always feel heavy. Like a slab of cement is on top of me.

"Please go rest!" I beg—but I know this ghost and the ghosts around me can't leave. I try to talk to them by saying:

"I'm sorry what happened to you—but I'm done carrying the weight of my mother, her father, and her father's father and everyone on both sides of my family tree!"

You see, I know there's so much generational trauma throughout our past. It's difficult to walk around knowing how much hurt happened. And I see you.

I see all of you.

I feel the pain. And I don't know how to help make It any better—but you all are suffocating the tranquility out of my life. And I have little, if any, **peace** left.

Be aware, I could leave you all behind, but that's not in my character. You know I believe in healing.

I believe in change.

But right now, I'm exhausted.

And the weight of our family's past, the history of the war within us—

With addiction, neglect, mental illnesses—I can go on and on.

But it's all too much for me to handle. I need help.

Ghost Story, Part Two

I need a sign.

A recognition.

Some divine intervention. God, give me a break—

Let me cry onto your shoulders.

I am afraid—the past is catching up to me.

God, I know I haven't talked to you in years . . .

You see, *I've* been walking in a graveyard in a place known to let the dead rest...

'Cause I'm trying to figure out how to make these ghosts of my past sleep in peace.

But every time I get a step closer, I am thrown away from where I need to be.

Like a piece of trash, I feel useless.

God, where are you? I am trying to find you. For the last few years, I have been angry with you, thinking that maybe you don't exist, but right now I have no other option than to call on you.

'Cause I feel hopeless and I have not found any one person or thing to help pull me out of this cycle I'm in, which leaves me feeling like my life is worth nothing. *Is my life worth nothing?*

I have tried attempting suicide in the past, but I'm scared that I'll end up in this same hell yet again.

So, I pray to you, God; I need you.

Please help me.

For I am too physically sick to be frightened, to be haunted . . . any longer.

I need peace of mind, body and soul.

God, will you help me?

I knew years in advance that it wasn't just a one-time deal. I remember at age 13, having to seek services. The school eventually spoke up, after I suffered panic attacks and crying spells during class.

I'm OK.

Then, out of nowhere, I'm OK. My security is taken. It can start with the anxiousness, where I feel everyone is staring at me and my clothes are too tight, the lights are too bright, and the sound is too loud.

I walk into a room and I'm overloaded. It's like my senses can't take it all in. There is far too much going on.

The thoughts come next; they remind me that everyone is watching me. I need to do things better. But it's a voice in my head, just a part of me that feels out of control.

But I continue doing what I am supposed to do. I go to work, maybe school, whatever . . . it gets worse. I fumble over my speech at work, and when I leave the house, I think people are judging me.

Finally, it comes, out of the blue—the suicidal thoughts. I could be anywhere, then I begin to think, *I should no longer be living*. I begin to believe the negativity in my head. I see every imperfection and exaggerate things to the core.

I convince myself that I need to be dead. That living is just too much. That I am not able to function, to be in control or do what I want to, so I should just leave and make it stop.

Lately, I've seemed to convince myself not to do it.

Even in my greatest despair, I've somehow kept going. After not killing myself, I usually want to get away or sleep, but the pain is still there. I'm haunted by my past. I see all the glimmers of the places I have been in my dark moments.

Sometimes, though, the lows, they hide. They sit below the surface for a while. I feel good for a bit, then I'm triggered by some random stimuli. I begin to break down. In the moment, I want to run away. I get angry, irritable, and I want to scream.

I get scared.

I need different medication.

My lithium needs to be increased, and I do not believe I'm on the right medication to control my thoughts and anxiety.

I believe these are combined a lot of the time.

My Xanax is good for panic attacks, but there is something the doctor gave me that may be better for what's going on with me, due to the general pattern within my episodes.

I take Trazodone to sleep, but it doesn't always work. I do not want to be on the sleeping pills.

I AM PSYCHOSIS PAINTING

A Picture of My Schizophrenia:

A Poem About My Psychosis

Spiders and bugs crawl into my ears at night—they lay eggs, then start a fight.

These creepy crawlers dig burrows throughout my body.

Killing every beautiful thing in sight till there's no light.

These bugs laugh at my hopes and dreams until they leave me with nothing.

I scream, I cry, I deny.

I wish my 13-year-old self didn't die.

I'm almost sure it was the rats that ate her.

Anyways she's dead and no longer is she in my head.

So, I need shut it up—

Let her rest in peace

Stomp feet and yell

God, can't you see I am suffering?

These creatures eat throughout my bones and brain—

That is when I feel the pain.

Dear God, it's me again, I am in so much pain.

Please take it away—I pray

As I go down the rabbit hole

I pull the remains of myself together.

I use crazy glue to try to paste the insides of

My body in place.

Oh God, please don't let me be a disgrace

These bugs are cruel—

Mixed up with depression and psychosis as fuel.

All I can do is wait. I set up ant traps and sticky tape—

All within my body—

To begin to trap these life-altering insects

I'll even start to fumigate.

I see a rat run across my feet

I don't know what to think

I blink.

He's gone.

He's dead.

Oh no!

That rat is chewing on the inside of my head

Gnawing on my brain

Infiltrating an area that makes me go insane.

This rat is the psychotic feature of my psychosis.

Stealing my reality as if it were a piece of cheese;

I fall to my knees.

God, oh—please make it stop!

Don't let the fear and anxiety knock me off my block!!!!

Fill my body with antipsychotics.

This pill better work better than that damn Hooked on Phonics!

I pray to you; do I get a reply?

Oh no, rat, please don't go for my eye.

I start to see red, please don't leave me for dead.

This rat is really hungry—

It gnaws at the core of my being.

But now I'm seeing the rat for what it really is . . .

A hallucination.

So let's make that provocation.

Please rise and pray with me.

Go away, rat—go away, rat, I'm kicking you out of my head.

Oops, now you're dead.

You have no control over me.

As you can see, I'm finally happy and healthy

Something I strive for each and every day.

Now I bow my head and say hello to the new me.

Let's hold our hands. Let's pray that rat is finally gone.

Dead out of my head

Maybe a day or two

Hopefully I'll get some rest from that hallucination

So I can enjoy life and pray for a miracle. A silent day and night

To recharge, to put up with the next fight.

I'll end those bugs right.

Ever-Consuming

I am disappointed. I'm afraid my anxiety and paranoia are consuming me. I am isolating myself from my friends. I no longer like going anywhere. I'm so sick of this; I am restless. I don't know what to do. Nothing is enjoyable anymore. I want to sleep. I want to sleep all day, so I don't have to feel life. Life is not living for me . . . life is terror. Life is pain. Life is ever-consuming fear.

Psychotic Episode

Psychotic Episode: where a person is out of touch with reality. Meaning they are seeing, hearing and feeling things that other people cannot experience (due to a mental illness, in my case, schizophrenia).

"You should just kill yourself already. No one loves you or cares about you. Oh, you see the scissors on your desk—yeah, those—slit your wrists."

Every day I wake up, I am bombarded by voices commenting on my every move. Urging me to kill myself, the voices tell me I am worthless. It takes me a good half hour to an hour to get out of my bedroom. I am petrified. Is someone watching me? Are people following me? What will happen if I open my bedroom door and a person is waiting for me with a knife? These are things I think about as I take my medications and prepare to take a shower.

I begin to lose my breath, my chest hurts and it feels like part of my air supply is being cut off. I am terrified to move from my bed. It takes every fiber of my being to leave my room and take a shower. I check the bathroom three times for the bad people. I am finally able to get into the shower. As I wash myself, the voices get louder—they tell me to drown myself. I start to get scared. While washing my hair, I start to hyperventilate. It feels like I can't breathe. My anxiety increases—I have to get out of the bathroom. I try to wash the shampoo out of my hair, but I don't get it all. I turn off the water as the voices comment about my breathing. I wrap a towel around my body, leaving the floor a water-soaked mess and I begin to cry. I run to my room and wrap blankets around me and cry until there are no more tears left.

Finally my medications kick in and I'm not as anxious as I was previously. I get dressed and get ready to go to a partial hospitalization program. As I wait to be picked up, I am on high alert. Looking out the window, I try to see if anyone is spying on me. I don't see anyone, but my senses tell me otherwise—the voices begin to tell me that other people are watching me from the windows.

As the hospital van gets to my house, I check the door to make sure it's locked and I get in. When I arrive at the program, I hear that the day's theme is gratitude—being thankful for all the things we have. The voices begin to say I am a rotten person and I don't deserve happiness. The thoughts in my head are disorganized and my depression ... well, my depression, it encapsulates my being.

How the fuck can I be thankful for anything—I lost my job, I totaled my car and toyed with the idea of being homeless.

And actually thought about telling my case manager I have a drug addiction and need a half-way house, so I don't have to rely on my friends to stay at their home. (Although I have never done street drugs of any kind.)

I have little family support and I'm living off a credit card. I have nothing to be thankful for. I want to die. I want to die peacefully in my sleep and feel nothing. I want the hopelessness gone and the voices to shut up. I want this pain to end. I'm just fucking overwhelmed with everything.

I begin to cry. I can't stop producing tears . . . No matter how much I try to stop crying, I can't. I hide my face so that no one can see me. I curl up into a ball and begin to rock myself. The whole room is silent—the group leader calls for someone to come talk to me. I try to get myself up off the couch as my whole body shakes. I haven't had proper sleep in two weeks, nor have I been eating regularly. My emotions are out of my control as I heave myself up off the couch.

I walk to the therapist's office and she offers a chair. I sit there and cry silently to myself as she takes notes. Asking me what triggered this . . . I tell her I am sorry, but I am not thankful for what I have—and I just want to die. I tell her about the voices, the pain, and she tells me she will be sending me to inpatient. I am scared. I tell her to please send me somewhere nice, but she says it's out of her hands where I get sent.

I'm so scared right now. I do not like the hospital. But I kind of know that I need to go there. The therapist starts notifying people that I need to be watched for the time being until the ambulance gets here. The therapist tells me to start calling my support system—to let them know I'm getting put in the hospital. I shake as I punch the numbers into my phone. I am going to get help.

ELECTRIC STORM PAINTING

I'm writing this looking back at the past, but talking about it as if it were the present.

I'm scared. I've been scared for a long time now. Years. I don't believe many people—if anyone—likes me. I feel like everyone is staring at me. Like I might collapse at any moment because of the weight of the pressure. It feels like people hate me and want me out of their lives. For dumb reasons, like looking at them too long. I'm scared to be around people in general. Social anxiety is horrible, plus this paranoia takes the cake. I hear people's thoughts. They tell me I don't belong here; they say to leave. I'm so confused. I don't know if people really like me or not.

Schizophrenia, I'm told by a therapist, is not easy to deal with.

I almost lost everything in my life, including my mind. I wasn't here; I was out of touch with reality so much, so I lost time. I couldn't tell you what happened in those days and it's probably better that I can't. But mental illness is no joke. This is one of the hardest parts to write in my book, because it shows how vulnerable I was at a point and how this illness can direct itself. But it is also one of the best parts of my story, because I've gained so much of my life back since then.

I deal with symptoms every single day, but my medications have changed since that period and therapists have changed and I'm feeling in control of my life. I've taken back control of crippling anxiety. It's still there, but not as tight.

I had to change the way I perceive the world through mindfulness techniques I learned. I had, and still have, to use grounding techniques to keep my anxiety in check and paranoia under way. Some days I can't do certain things and I have to respect my mind and body; other days, I'm able to do more.

The grounding techniques involve your senses of taste, touch, sight, sound, smell and feeling. When you are in an anxious state or are slipping into psychosis, for example, sometimes you can use your senses to calm yourself and bring yourself to center and reality. Otherwise, finding distractions is helpful.

Being scared to be alive is the loneliest feeling I've ever felt. If you ever feel like that, please know you are not alone. There are other people out there who are in the same boat. It can get better. Please believe me. It can. I am with you. I am by your side.

I've been disorganized. All over the place lately. With an "I don't care" attitude. I'm just sick of everything. I feel worn out. This school semester has dragged on for too long.

Sometimes, I get in my car and just think about ending it all, right then and there. Other days I think about all my pills and say to myself, *Why not?*

I don't appear depressed, sad, to others. I'm not feeling those things; I just have been real low, real down. My hope is decreasing.

I can feel the life in my veins running slower.

My passions are dwindling and I just want to quit.

I'm sick of fighting.

I feel like I have been through a boxing match for far too long without a break. I never got enough time to calm down from the highs or lows, nor the anxiety before the match.

Now I just feel like I'm left cold, naked and exposed in this ring of life. Fighting for survival in a match that was originally given to me, is produced from my environment, and now lives within my being.

Education, Hopes & Dreams

I passed my classes. I'm not sure how that occurred. It seems like this has become a pattern for me, which is scary.

It feels like every semester is becoming more and more of a fight.

NERVES PAINTING

I'm kind of terrified to see what will happen after I do graduate from college. I need to go to grad school, but I feel like I am getting weaker.

I want to not care.

I'm tired.

I hate living with myself.

Every day I feel more detached from everyone. I wish I could be like them, but I just fall further down.

I feel like I am unable to be who I want to be, to love or be loved, because I am a broken, untrusting person.

I want so badly to live free from these demons. Within my mind, they are so negative.

I will tell you that I do feel like there is a part of me, a healthy part, still left. Unfragmented, it's small, compact, but sturdy. Buried under all the darkness, growing with hope, this piece of me stays intact.

I know she is there. I see her light; it is just hard when the dark gets darker and the heavy gets heavier.

I still have hopes and dreams. Even amongst the darkness, I am wishing, hoping and praying to stay alive. I desperately want to live. I want to achieve my goals. I want to survive. I want to be someone someday. I want to impact a life. I want to help others. Possibly make a difference in this world.

I went to college and served two terms in AmeriCorps, including participation on a child abuse prevention council where I conducted mandated reporter trainings. I helped teach English as a second language to at-risk preschoolers, and taught them how to read the alphabet, write and gain other early literacy skills.

I also worked as a Youth Advocate for a non-profit agency where I told my mental health story about growing up in the system. I did this to show other youth and young adults that they are not alone in their struggles. This agency was part of a youth-led leadership initiative in Detroit, Michigan and Wayne County (where Detroit is located) called Youth United, which helps teens and young adults come together and share their journeys through different systems of care for mental health, juvenile justice and developmental disabilities. Youth United employs young adults touched by these systems to learn about policy change, ways to reduce the stigma of mental illness, leadership skills, and much more.

In addition to Youth United, I had the privilege to work with Youth Move National—a youth-driven, chapter-based organization across America that helps lessen the stigma of mental illness and other disorders. It brings young people together to create policy change and other systems of reform, by listening to young people who experienced different systems. In this instance, I participated in a Youth Move chapter and talked about my experiences to help create changes for the future.

Now that I have graduated from the University of Michigan-Dearborn with a degree from the interdisciplinary program in Behavioral Science from the College of Arts, Sciences and Letters, I want to help with policies regarding mental health and I want to be in a position to inspire youth and young adults to receive the best services possible. I need to attend graduate school, possibly earning a master's degree in social work.

My Angels, Grey and Joy

Grey and Joy are my roommates. We met during my freshman year of college. They are partners and have literally looked out for me and saved my life countless times. I can't just classify them as roommates or even friends. They are real-life angels who go above and beyond what is normal. They are people who care, who are selfless, and who were willing to help me at my complete lowest state of functioning. They are incredible to me and will always and forever hold a special place in my heart.

They are the people who removed all the sharp objects from the house, the individuals who gave me my medication during certain periods when I needed help taking it. They let me sleep on their bedroom floor when I was too paranoid to sleep in my bedroom. And they checked my closet for monsters when I was visually hallucinating. I can't give my angels enough credit for everything they have done for me. Because most of the time, I didn't even ask them to do the things they did; they just did them to help me. I love those guys!

Besides these two individuals, I was lucky to have two friends who always had my back. Preetii and Sarah. Preetii always made me laugh and gave me happiness. She was a ray of sunshine and always helped me on short notice. I didn't appreciate her enough. Sarah was someone I worked with; she helped me get closer to my higher power. She was very kindhearted. I was and am fortunate to have close friendships. These people all helped me tremendously throughout college and after. Unfortunately, I ruined the relationship I had with Preetii. I ended up writing an apology. I truly hope she finds peace and happiness; she deserves it.

A Loud Poem

Dedicated to my Grandma

"Speak up," she says
"I can't hear you,
you know
you speak too softly!"
"Gram!"
I yell into my cellphone—
"Can you hear me?"
"I can hear you,
a little better," she says.

My grandma tells me the weather up there—as she lives in northern Michigan—and her plans for the day. She talks about her health and asks me what's been happening with me in the Metro Detroit area—a place she grew up in and misses dearly. She is and will always be a (proud) Detroiter . . .

I tell my gram, my best friend, my gram cracker, that I'm well.

And I miss her.

I miss seeing her on a daily basis. I miss her hugs, her smile, and even her random singing . . . in Polish and English.

I tell her she knows exactly what to say to get me from falling into a deep abyss or well that I can't imagine surviving . . .

Another tragedy or loss, my grandma reminds me of my past encounters with the dark corners of life and of one's mind.

Telling me it'll be OK, because it always is. In the end— as long as we survive.

We have the opportunity to keep going.

I am my gram's granddaughter—

I have her mental illnesses locked up in my soul—I walk in her painful footsteps on hard times; I am just realizing that I am like her. A little wild for others, yet at times painfully quiet. Our moods go up and down—like our thoughts race—we are one of a kind.

"Gram—" I ask, "how am I going to get through the suicidal thoughts, this car wreck, the job loss, my physical pain from this illness, the mental anguish. I am worried I will end up homeless . . . Grandma, I am lost." I plead to her over the years. I am out of options.

"Bethany," she says, "get up off your feet and listen to me. You were born too early. I could fit you in the palm of my hands—baby doll, you were and are so incredibly precious to me. You survived many situations you don't even remember and you were on all these monitors in the intensive care unit—we didn't know what was going to happen. But you came home."

I listen to my grandma's voice; deep in my heart, I know she's right.

My grandma is a warrior. I see her life painted on her skin—she went through hell, lived in hell—and eventually returned after fighting with the devil himself. My grandma is no joke. She helped raise me up to believe that anything can be possible—dreams can come true. But suffering is also a reality, and we must always be thankful for what we have. My grandma is a survivor and fighter.

Her early life was not easy, she tells me. She grew up in the Great Depression. She gives me insight into her whole life, the pains and beauty. My Gram tells me to celebrate the good. She tells me to speak up when I need help. To not be afraid of certain things, like she is.

"Bethany," she says, "I'm so glad you can use your voice, because I wish I could have used mine in similar situations. Girl, keep going. I can't hear you. Speak up! Speak louder—"

"I will, Gram," I shout into the phone.

"Grandma," I say, "I need to tell you something before we get off the phone." I enunciate every syllable and say every word as loud as I can—

"Grandma, my Gram, my gram cracker. You are my sunshine. Like the lullaby you sang to me as a kid.

"I need you to know how much warmth you bring into my life when I had no concept of such lighthearted beauty.

"Today, you are the reason I now know how to bring out my own sunshine. And I will always remember that it was you who taught me how to do this—as well as pray, dream, and find light within the places I could only imagine darkness.

"Thank you.

"Let me say it louder—just in case you can't hear me—thank you! Thank you!"

THE LAUNDRY LIST

all the medications I have taken since age 13

I've taken so many medications, I tend to lose count.
Paxil,
Klonopin,
Trazodone,
Zyprexa,
Risperdal,
Depakote,
Latuda,
Prozac,
Wellbutrin,
Effexor,
Abilify,
Geodon,
Brintellix,
Xanax,
Seroquel,
Cymbalta,
Lunesta,
Trintellix,
Adderall,
Concerta,

Ativan,

Valium,

Zoloft,

Remeron,

Buspar,

Lithium,

Prolixin,

Tegretol,

Ambien,

Minipress,

and Saphris . . .

That's 33 that I can remember, and I'm sure I've taken more.

Well, a few weeks ago, I had to go to the crisis center again. I needed some help. I started hallucinating. Seeing things again, but this time, really bad. It scared me. I was very fearful.

I saw this long rope hanging from the ceiling. This image haunts me. Reminds me of a noose. It kept appearing. I also saw a man in a closet. I thought he was going to kill me. There were other things, like objects that appeared to be melting, but they didn't bother me as much as those stated above.

UP IN SMOKE PAINTING

When I got to the crisis center this time, I got put on a 23-hour hold, meaning they kept me overnight. It was very boring, but I was scared. I didn't know what to expect.

I was nervous sleeping somewhere I had never slept before, around people I didn't know.

Right now, my life, my survival, are in another person's hands.

You see, I'm screaming.

PART III

SCREAMING . . . HELP!

SCREAMING . . . HELP!

I'm screaming for someone to save me—as if I'm in a body of water and I don't know how to swim—I need help, I say. There's a person to the left of me who turns around and looks at me. I've never seen them before this moment and they just observe me—struggling to keep my head above the water—they are three feet away and they have a life vest next to them. They could throw me this vest at any time . . . but am I worth . . . saving?

Saving: it's to give a person with a disability a sum of money per month and health insurance so they can keep their head above the water to survive and live.

To be saved, you have to convince the system/social security disability that you meet certain requirements and can no longer work. There's more to it, but the gist is that they must see the person—or, in this case, me—not only struggle to survive each and every single day— which I do—-with multiple mental and physical health problems, but they also have to witness that I feel like the illness(s) will last for X amount of time.

So, the question is, *Am I worth saving?* I currently have social security disability and Medicare—but I'm up for review . . . and my life will change drastically if I lose them, because I can't work.

I won't be able to pay for my medications. There's 21 of them and eight are psychiatric. You see, I couldn't function at all without them—I might end up dead or seriously hurt without my psychiatric medications and services, to be honest . . . do you see my rap sheet? I've attempted suicide multiple times and have experienced quite a bit of trauma, but at the end of the day, is my mental and physical pain worth anything at all? Does living in terror count for the precious pennies I hope to keep getting?

You see, I have PTSD (Post Traumatic Stress Disorder), schizoaffective disorder, depression and anxiety, and ADHD (attention-deficit/hyperactivity disorder). When my psychosis acts up, I experience bouts of paranoia with agoraphobia (extreme fear of leaving home). And that's just my mental health.

My physical health is deteriorating, too.

From interstitial cystitis (painful bladder syndrome), fibromyalgia (a disorder that causes pain everywhere, exhaustion and insomnia) and migraines, it's hard to move my body some days or leave my room due to light sensitivity and pain.

But the real question—is my life worth prolonging?

Is my life worth saving?

You see, my life is in a stranger's hands—a person I've never seen or met—and I'm screaming for help . . . I'm screaming for help . . .

Because I will not be able to survive without disability income and health insurance . . . so, how much does it cost to save a person like myself?

Because at the end of the day, it's about money and I'm just another number . . .

So will they save a number—I mean, me?

Will they save me?

I Chose Life

I am unsure that you are aware of what I just did. I chose to not give in.

I chose to stay above the ground.

I fought the monster inside me and I won. Never thinking that moment was possible, beating hopelessness, because that's the thing that kills people like me.

It's the pain and suffering that all we all feel.

And this is our life—people with mental illness . . . they struggle. And you can't see it, so most people dismiss it.

They have no idea what it's like to feel like you have nothing left.

Nothing.

It's despair—yet, you can't see it, so it's not there.

People who never experienced it have no idea what pain is. The pain of contemplating your own life—deciding if it's time to die. Have you ever been on the edge of life or death?

You probably haven't, but I'll give you the benefit of the doubt; It's a day where you decide if you can live with the monster inside.

And let me tell you, it's not very easy. Yet I survived.

I am a survivor, and nobody knows.

I fought a battle against myself and won,

Not just one time, but countless times.

I am a fighter. I am someone who can persevere. Because I am strong.

And it's my job to defend myself.

To allow myself to die when I'm supposed to.

Car Ride

It's just another Tuesday and . . .

My mind is running laps around a track my brain made to drive *me* to a destination with no exit.

I find myself in the fetal position.

You see,

I'm trying to survive my life.

An experience that I don't always want to engage in, but am at times forced to try and retry to recharge and give it a jump—because I tend to break down.

My car's got the gas light on E. It's So Empty, like my hands.

My hands and feet hurt all the time. The pain rises and rises—goes up throughout my body. My body is betraying the parts that I thought would not rust for many years.

My oil is almost nonexistent.

You see, I need to stop immediately

Before I crash into a heap of hopelessness

You see, I'm sick of getting bitten

By my own chemically imbalanced and traumatized mind. But I'm going to have to work.

Work every single day on myself.

I will put gas in my car, go to therapy and give myself a hug. Doing what I can, with what I have-

Even if it's just another Tuesday.

I'll check myself instead of wrecking me and what I have.

Because there is no way I'm going to fall in line with a destination that has been trying to destroy

All the precious work

I put in to erase everything I fought so hard to get. My strength may waver. But I will not give up, even if it's just me riding in my car, in my car on just another plain Tuesday.

My Body, My Prison Cell

Sometimes, I take a seat in my bedroom and try to think of something to do. I sit for hours at a time. Sometimes, I don't realize how long I just sit. When I am overwhelmed, I'll shut down and can't think of anything—I feel like I'm wasting time, but end up doing nothing anyway. At times, I'll catch myself talking to myself.

Thoughts of suicide enter my mind on and off. I have had them since I started reading in elementary school. I didn't know what they were; I just wished and prayed that I wouldn't wake up to see the next day, because that would mean I was still alive.

The suicidal thoughts come throughout my life; some days, I think I am triggered by something—they are very strong and last from a few hours to a few days. When I am depressed, they can last months.

I am very jumpy, easily scared. I jump out of my chair from the smallest noise. At night, this is not good because I wake up easily, ready to get up and throw a punch and/or run. I have awakened my boyfriend recently because of this, as well as from nightmares related to trauma.

I am extremely sensitive to light, sounds and tem-peratures. I have a really difficult time going to crowded public places. I have to take a nap after going to the store. I am exhausted physically and mentally.

After grocery shopping or even getting my haircut—if there are bright lights, or lots of people, it's hard for me to focus and I get overwhelmed. Sometimes I get paranoid being around all those people. I think they are watching me closely. There are times where I leave the store because it's too loud or bright for me and I can't finish shopping. Or I get a panic attack because I feel that in my head I am being told no one wants me at the store, and everyone is talking about me in a bad way ('cause I can hear them think).

Clothing textures also bother me at times. I am very picky about fabric and how it feels.

Some days, I'll change up to five times.

The first outfit takes the most time. It's weird—it's like all of a sudden, I have no idea where to start or what to do on my (bad) days.

I sit and stare at my dresser sometimes for 30 or more minutes—not knowing what to do . . . my mind goes blank.

Some days, it takes me more than three hours to get ready to leave the house, when really it should take 45 minutes. I've had this issue since I was a young girl—I get lost in my head. I don't know what to do next. Mornings are rough; I wake up anxious. And I feel shaky on the inside. It's hard to hold myself together.

I've been through various traumatic experiences throughout my life and I still have issues with trust, safety and the aftereffects.

I have impulse issues at times—usually when I haven't slept for a few days, or during periods of time with psychosis or manic mood.

Examples include: overeating or undereating, overspending, doing artwork or writing for days without rest, doing risky activities, etc.

During each day, I ruminate often on thoughts that torture me . . . I obsess on things that have happened previously. I live with physical pain that haunts me all day. With migraines and pain in my feet—most days I can hardly get exercise due to neuropathy (nerve damage) in my feet, hands and body . . . it's too painful to walk as much as I want to.

I have bladder problems (on bad days, I go to the bathroom every 20 minutes). On top of this, I'm having a hard time sitting for periods of time. Every hour or so it feels like my butt is in too much pain to sit normally on a chair due to neuropathic pain and fibromyalgia. I also live with asthma and tachycardia.

And through all this, I feel broken.

But I still want calmness in my body and in my life. I know somehow, one day, I can and will feel better. I just need time and healing. I go to a urologist for help on some of these issues—I talk to my therapist and eventually things get not as cumbersome. I am respecting my body even through my manic episodes; I'm in a better relationship and feeling more functional in many regards. I am seeing a neurologist for my small fiber neuropathy and I am using different strategies for my chronic pain, such as TENS units (a small device that relieves pain by sending small electrical currents to body parts) and heating pads. I am seeing a cardiologist and using breathing treatments.

Suicide

My greatest fear is that I'll end up killing myself. I'm 24 years old.

Sometimes I think about it and can't believe it. I can't believe I'm still here.

I thought I would have chosen to end my life by now.

I remember my first bout of depression at 13 and thinking then and there, if this mental anguish were to continue, I would be dead by 18.

I'm telling you this because it's important. **The hardest thing I have ever had to do in my life was to live, when the only thing I ever wanted to do was die.** I wish I could tell you how strong you have to be to choose life.

Every day I hide from my illness—

In a show that I perform for you and the masses. I let my outer appearance distract you from the pain I am in. Controlled by the strings of a deranged and cognitively impaired puppet master, I cover up the symptoms of my mental illness.

So, our story begins . . .

I play the part of a 24-year-old, college-educated woman. Living with three roommates whom I call family.

I try my hardest to fit in, when all I want to do is isolate. I paint my face with colors to look alive. I force myself to laugh when my body is stone cold.

As my ability to relate to others diminishes, you might begin to see the monster I'm trying to hide. Flashes of an insect—mangled in front of you, trigger you to look away.

No one wants to see what's hiding under the mask I wear.

So, when my pain leaks out, I immediately try to change your sight of these damaged interactions—I then swiftly turn back into the character I am playing. I remind myself again of who I am.

I am an insect, torn apart and crushed together by two shards of glass displayed under a lighted microscope. Held together by two strings, moving my insect body like a mobile.

Everyone can see me.

I am in pieces.

I am a prisoner locked in a place worse than any physical prison cell. For I am a prisoner of my mind. Manipulated not only by my illness, but by the little faith of reality I hold to be true.

I start my days off by waking up to the living hell that my mind has created for me.

I am immediately overwhelmed . . .

Whether by voices, noises, anxiety or sheer panic, I sit on the edge of my bed and listen to my heart beat as I begin to fly off the handle. I need to sit and breathe.

Conversing is a puzzle. I put words like popcorn on a string to be hung on a Christmas tree together. The popcorn being words—light and easily breakable—at times falling apart (with each piece, I form sentences).

I have to concentrate; my memory is fading due to disorganized thoughts. Faces, words and numbers look foreign to me.

I can't spell words I used to know. I forget who people are—people in my distant family, old co-workers, etc.

My phone can't even spell check some of the words I type. I pace.

I have a hard time sitting still.

Sometimes, I see people and things appear out of the darkened recesses of my head. These particular people are hallucinations.

However, my reality amongst the living promotes fear.

I have a hard time relating to others, as now my identity has changed. My authentic self has left me. She has been gone for 12 years. I mourn her. You can now only see glimmers of her when my heart opens and my eyes light up . . . which now happen days and months far and in between. Now you mostly see a flat affect or practiced smile carved out of my face like a Jack-'o-lantern—reinforced by the part of my mind that still understands societal norms.

People scare me. Parties, new and public places, new faces, all make my body twist and contort as I try to fit in.

Remember, I am under that microscope and people are watching. Paranoia ensues.

Listening to others' thoughts I hear, I am stealing, I'm dirty, I am a waste of space. I am loud . . .

Sometimes I hear other voices commenting on what I'm doing . . . while others tell me to kill myself. I try my best not to listen to what goes on in my head. I pray to be present.

I want to live in the moment. I want to change the world. I wanted to do many things . . .

Are you beginning to see what my mind has stolen from me?

My mind has taken a chunk of my life away . . . no longer can I say, "I'll remember this moment;" no longer can I say confidently, "I will own a home one day;" no longer can I say, "I'll have children;" no longer can I say, "I'll be able to go back to school."

No, I have mini goals, goals I can accomplish for that day—goals like getting up and fixing my hair.

I didn't know an illness could steal parts of your life away. Never was I taught what to do if your own mind is working against you.

So, I ask of you this favor . . . as the play comes to an end . . . help me live alongside my illness. Please help me when the fire comes and goes, to be there for me. To never give up on me—to know I am indeed a fighter. I may turn into a monster occasionally or display one of my broken wings, but you now know why. I'm the strongest person I know.

Grace

There is nothing left to see here, ladies and gentlemen—

I'm going to have to ask you again to please leave—and return to your homes.

Caution—they say this is a place you do not want to be. I'll say this one more time, the voice pleads to the crowd, Go home.

Like the sketch on the pavement of what and who I used to be isn't already a sign of war within my being. I do not fit in this space and I pray to the God(s) I never do.

People love to stop and gawk at the wreckage of strangers. I mean, really, anyone—except when it comes to themselves . . . because empathy and humanity are becoming too out of style . . . not representative of our individualistic culture of this great place of freedom . . .

You see, I tried to tell you that I needed help. That I screamed for attention because the level of my pain could be compared to nothing I had ever experienced.

Like the time he threw knifes straight down to my soul—where only beauty and grace lived and I saw him kill Grace with his filthy fucking hands around her neck...

Yeah, I saw you.

That day, I screamed so hard, I felt my lungs burn.

Looking back, I told you I'd get my revenge. You see, I don't leave anything unfinished or anyone behind . . . but you shattered a part of me and I am going to get her back one way or another.

Grace! I screamed. I'm here for you, dear, and I'm ready to dig every unmarked grave out of this monster's collection of people he tried to kill—but I'm here now, honey, and so are Kim and Bridget. And together we will get your body out of this disgusting hell hole.

You are worth so much, Grace, do you hear us? Grace, you are precious and kind.

I will not ask what happened.

I will not pry.

I will try not to cry.

But you look terrified.

You look scared.

The kind you can't unsee

To rip off the broken skin and keep going. It's me that's running, it's you I'm chasing, and it's time to stop racing . . . Grace, I'm here.

I'm sorry

I'm making this destruction

That's fueled by the fire—I mean trauma of everything I can and can't remember. Please, please, Grace, forgive me. Or at least stop running. I am exhausted.

So, I know you have to be exhausted even more.

Bethany, it's Grace,

Stop running.

I am not going anywhere.

Look in any mirror and you will see me.

Look closer if you need to—remember I am a part of you and I'm not leaving.

Look, the trauma cannot control you or me or all of us. I need you to stop—stop going to the house.

The place that could have killed us.

Be aware—keep your eyes open.

Stay alert.

And put the gun down.

You will not pull the trigger.

This is not going to be the end of you, of us—

You will not have your body drawn on the pavement

like some kind of fucked up reminder that you died because the trauma was too heavy for your heart to hold and the Depression too bitter—because you were alone. Girl, stop it.

The chalk won't show your beautiful long hair or pretty brown eyes.

Girl, calm yourself, we are here for you!! And the monsters are gone.

No one will hurt you.

Put the weapon down and listen—

You are not to live in the ashes, the shadows, the grave, that you dug yourself to rot and die in.

This place is for the dead to rest and you were never asked or welcomed here.

So, stop pleading, stop arguing with death. I know it hurts to talk and breathe at times, but you still have time.

You are alive, do you hear me?

You are alive.

Preserve your time.

Leave, girl.

Be a stranger to this neighborhood, this graveyard, this coffin, this hell on Earth—and breathe.

Breathe.

Breathe again and again.

Honey.

Leave now.

PART IV

Learning to
Find Hope

WAR PAINTING

LEARNING TO FIND HOPE

8/2

I don't know what it is about today, but I'm really paranoid. I tried going to church, but I had to leave early. I just feel like all these people are watching me. I'm extremely uncomfortable. I have this yearning to go hide in my room. I want it to stop. I feel so exposed. Like every single person is watching me.

8/10

Sometimes I just want to give up. I just don't know what to do.

9/8

I had another day with the monsters in my head. I keep thinking my life isn't worth living due to the current circumstance. I have no job, no school, no anything to fill my day, except for support groups. But I need these support groups; they keep me together.

9/9

I wish you knew how much strength it takes just to get up in the morning.

9/9

Today is the day I'm supposed to be on this youth panel to discuss suicide. It's also World Suicide Prevention Day. And I feel a little confused giving this talk because the past couple of days I have felt suicidal.

You know what? Fuck it. I'm done with this bullshit. I'm taking my life back. Fuck you, mental illness! I'm not allowing you to take me prisoner anymore. My mind is mine and I'm in control. I am my own person. I will not be defined by my mental illness. I am a person first, diagnosis second. So, fuck you, insomnia! Fuck you, paranoia! Fuck you, depression! You are not taking my life anymore.

9/10

Today I got to talk about my mental health struggles for World Suicide Prevention Day at a local CMH (Community Mental Health services organization). It was great—some people even commented on my stigma video. You can watch the video by searching online for: r e s i l i e n c e // Youth United // [Documentary] // Detroit.

9/14

Today I volunteered in the clothing room at a mental health agency. I really enjoyed it. I also like their groups. My favorite is a self-esteem group.

Looking back at the last few years of my life, I can see profound changes in my core that I couldn't notice until very recently.

Changes that almost took my life and ripped it apart. If not for my doctor, I don't know where I'd be. I dedicate this story to Dr. K, my psychiatrist, the person who saw me when I needed help the most and continues to this day to help me face things no human should have to endure, but nonetheless does. Thank you, Dr. K.

These last few years, I have drifted away from being an optimistic, bubbly, vivacious person to being an introverted, scared and withdrawn individual. Life feels heavy, it feels disorganized and scattered, and my mind is cluttered.

You see, I am a college graduate with a bachelor's degree, but I can no longer concentrate to read a book. Thank goodness I can still write. But often my mind feels foggy.

However, this past year was really hard for me in particular. I thought the people closest to me were plotting against me. I thought they didn't love me and didn't care about me. And I constantly thought they were planning on kicking me out of their house when, in reality, they weren't.

I became frightened and began inquiring about this and it only made them confused and frustrated. As things in my mind escalated, I believed the government was also conspiring against me and that my boyfriend's family didn't like me and wanted me gone.

At this point, I ended up at a crisis center where I saw my doctor, Dr. K. We had already tried changing my medications two times before I made it here, but I could barely think straight.

Nothing made sense. I thought the TV was talking to me; I thought my cell phone was tracked. And I heard voices constantly. But Dr. K didn't give up on me. Almost as soon as I got to the crisis center, I had a severe mental breakdown. I heard and saw all these government officials arresting me. I was terrified and thought the only way to survive was to say certain phrases over and over. I don't remember much more than that, but I was in pure terror.

I finally broke out of the mental anguish . . . and talked to

Dr. K. I started taking medication and was sent to a hospital.

Dr. K has been my doctor for years now. I trust him. He has helped me transform my life in a multitude of ways since leaving the hospital.

I still live with schizoaffective disorder, but I'm learning to manage it. I don't deal with the same symptoms as I used to. Things are different. It's still difficult. I am learning coping strategies. One that has helped a lot is listening to music. Music has been a life changer, along with psychiatry.

We live with new changes every day; what matters is how we approach them. Things are going to happen, no matter what. But we have to be prepared to shift our thinking and move forward. Dr. K taught me that.

Thank you, Dr. K. You continue to not only enrich my life, but also to educate me on the things I need to survive with this stubborn illness. You are sincerely appreciated.

Lost Dreams

I no longer make plans.

I no longer think of the future I once thought I could have.

I wanted everything. I wanted so much. I desperately wanted to be successful.

I go day to day, surviving.

Each and every day is new; I never know which monsters will keep popping up.

All I know is that this will keep happening.

They tell me I have a chronic mental illness. They tell me this will be a part of my life forever and I will have to learn how to gauge when enough is enough.

I really want to help people. I really want to work with at-risk kids and teenagers. I want to do great things.

But what happens when your illness hinders your actions?

I went to college. I worked hard and received a bachelor's degree in Behavioral Science.

I want to be a social worker.

I want to change the world . . . and sometimes I still think I can.

Scream

Suddenly out of the darkened recesses inside my being, something primitive is triggered—and I see myself helpless and hear my conscience plead. For a second, traumatic memories flood over me. I don't want to see the pain—I want it to stop—I want her to stop screaming. It's too much—it's all too much. I'm in past places—I don't want to be or see or relive this and I realize in the moment that she is actually a part of me—and she has been there this whole time so I can cope and survive.

So why do I see her? Why do I feel drawn to her? How is this going to end?

The screaming gets louder and, for the first time in my life, I discover that it's me—

I am that wild woman who can't. Stop. Screaming.

Poem

I am living in a cage

A body

A holy place

A broken temple

A crime scene

A prison

That is falling apart

Decaying

And decomposing like the garbage left on the street.

I am too tired to sweep myself up.

Do you see me clearly?

'Cause—

There is so much more to my story than the last week's makeup I have drawn on my face.

A disguise

A coping mechanism

A lie

Something I have to do to go outside

Until I melt away

Like Sunday's snowfall

You see,

My outer shell is a canvas.

I will never allow anyone to peek under my skin. My armor has been baptized, but it's also been educated. I pray for scientific breakthroughs. I work my own 12 steps.

Steps an old soul like me has to take.

Slowly and carefully . . . 'cause I know what's coming around the corner. I've seen this 100 times.

This is the way my body is designed—it wants to hide . . . Under the mattress with all the broken mirrors full of Kleenex and tears. But it cannot fit in such a tight space, so it hides in the closet and tries to erase everything that made it a disgrace.

If only it had a clue that its inner child was crying at a great pace. Needing just love to help it feel that her feelings were indeed validated and real. Let's get this child's cage to come undone and get her holiness to be praised once again.

Heavy

This poem is going to be heavy.

Like the burden, I carry it everywhere I go. These words drop from my teeth, showing those around me what I am attempting to digest. These symptoms are akin to what I tolerate, what I must endure; they cling to my being like nothing any human has seen before me.

I am a person who *strives* for inner peace. Me. I am Bethany. And this poem is, and has, been killing me. Silently, like a heart attack. Living on my chest. The killer has been in me for the last few months and I need my body to be freed from this beast so I can finally breathe again.

And, no, I am not suicidal; I am not the killer. The killer is paranoia; it's delusional and has multiple voices. It distorts my thinking and destroys who I am as a person. It's anxiety, it's rumination—it's PTSD.

However, remember, I am Bethany. I will always fight for myself. But, like this poem says, I carry this burden everywhere I go, because life gets heavy. Good thing I've got coping skills and strong supports, 'cause I know how to use them and will, even if they are a bit weighty.

I need my lifelines. Also known as my lovelines. And because I know I'm exhausting, my lovelines need their supporters as well.

And I need help destroying the monster trying to squeeze the Bethanyness out of me. I'm not myself when I'm like this.

I'm blank.

I'm wiped out.

I'm exhausted.

I don't care.

Maybe I'm terrified, maybe I'm confused . . .

But maybe, just maybe, I also need to remember I'm not the burden.

A Love Letter to the One Who Sees Me as I Am: a Person, Not a Diagnosis.

This is a love letter written to you, Jer, from me. This is more than any proclamation or explanation of one's truest feelings you have ever heard.

This is written out of all the tears I've cried, dreams I've lost, and people who have left me.

This is the lockbox holding the key to what and who made me who I am today.

This is the happiness that drove the madness away.

This is HOPE, the HOPE of what the future may bring. The bright light of your eyes that brings me peace.

This is *my* joy to you, and I have always meant you, Jer.

My dear, you are destined for greatness. You are loved beyond measure and this is the sign you've been looking for. This is the missing beat of the drum within my soul beating for you.

The drum of your heart, the rhythm of your pulse. Your pulse, yes, you.

You, my love, are alive. You are here on this beautiful, chaotic place we call home.

Yes, we are together; and in your arms, I am **home.**

You've told me, my love, you feel alone at times,

But you see, you are here with me and I'm here to remind you that I will be by your side.

Jer, love is power and love is the *only* power that can extinguish the poison that infiltrates our being from what we are truly worth.

Jer, you are worth more than the stars in the sky. My love, this is more than a love letter.

This, my love, is just the beginning.

An Apology, a Reason to Live

Dear Bethany,

This is my declaration to you.

The one you deserved forever ago as an awakening, an apology and a reason to keep breathing.

You see, it's me.

I'm the piece and part of you that broke off in order to survive . . . and I'm coming to you today to say I'm sorry.

I'm sorry for how I acted,

For how I took care of myself,

For how I talked to you.

And I just want to—

I just want to hold you in my arms and cradle you. I want to sing to you—

Sing our song,

The one about the sun.

Sing you are my sunshine, my little sunshine.

But we are no longer little and our lives are cloudy and I am so sick of being stuck in the rain. Cause weather doesn't change where I am. And it is your pain that placed me/trapped me in this spiderweb of thunder clouds.

And I know you didn't mean to put me here. Survival can be cruel.

Bethany, I know you are often misunderstood as a person and I get it.

But what I don't comprehend is when you tried to kill me.

You tried to kill us. What does that say about the medications, the therapy that we consume on the daily?

Are you really working the program? Because I am.

OK, please forgive me, I know you were and are still fighting every single day to get better.

It's like this:

It seems no matter what happens, we keep getting so sick when we feel hell's fire on this beautiful planet we call home when we did nothing wrong.

When we are survivors of unspoken memories—yet we

are punishing ourselves . . . that doesn't make any sense.

Sometimes I think of Einstein:

He once said knowledge is limited; imagination encircles the world.

I know creativity saved me as a child,

Maybe it'll help now as an adult.

You see, I am starting to believe in the power of art to heal, just like getting a little sunlight.

It just feels right. Maybe one day, healing will feel alright.

Just like self-preservation.

I will not let you become another tragic loss.

You see, I'm sick of seeing potential get eaten by the worms in the ground of burial plots.

As they said in the perks of being a wallflower,

"I will not be another sad story."

I will not let you fall into the depths of pain that play within your brain, trying to succumb to the inner peer pressure of suicidal thoughts and actions.

It's not going to happen.

But if it does, I will remind you,

How incredible it is to be in this moment after surviving so much. Keep going. You may find the best day of your life is yet to come.

And just being here is a celebration that you made it.

Because, as I said before, you are my sunshine, my only sunshine, and it is you that makes me—

Happy when my skies are gray.

And I know you can't see me, but I am in your heart.

The part of you that broke off,

You kept whole.

And you saved yourself, girl.

Keep going. Keep going.

Because you are your own sunshine,

And that in itself is the reason to be alive.

Forgiveness

How do we forgive ourselves for the things we did not become?

I have wrestled with my identity for the last decade. I put all my effort into becoming the "best" person I could be . . . I wanted to be successful and I thought that higher academia, perfectionism and God would allow me to rise higher than my parents; for, as a young person, I had unrealistic standards and thought that these actions would help me establish my goals.

You see, I mastered the art of hiding my mental illnesses or, should I say, trying to act like what a "normal" person in my eyes/life experiences would be like. As a teenager/young adult, I teeter-tottered back and forth from a goth to a nerd to a character out of a fantasy show due to my manic phases. Never able to land on a "good" character to play, I relied on my eyes to get me by. My eyes taught me to try to predict other people's body movements, helping me to pick out the people I thought at the time would hurt me.

Unfortunately, I was born with "the crossed eyes." I had and still have never been able to "see" myself correctly, so how would I know how to portray anyone else when the glasses I had didn't work? And the people that were closest to me acted on their addictions. So, my identity was difficult to see—all I really saw were ghosts of my broken dreams.

Like I mentioned before, I had unrealistic standards. And I realized that I had failed myself after losing job after job, time after time—times when I had little, if any control over my circumstances—because I hadn't accepted that the voices in my head were real. Yes, I was living with real hallucinations that did, and still do, reside in my brain that broke down many years ago with no signs of repair.

I had to come to the reconciliation that no number of prayers or medications could or would fix me.

Yes, preacher. Yes, doctor. I had tried to talk to you both.

I now recognize that medicine from my doctor helped quiet and tame *some* of the mental abuse I experience/d every single second of my day; and, preacher, you had only told me a million times to keep going to penance, telling me to keep confessing my sins. I had waited many years to be "saved" and am no longer afraid of purgatory when I live/d in hell.

You see, I get real—I get real tripped up when terrorized for extended periods of time by chemical imbalances and trauma, which my identity for the longest has held on to. Maybe I need another antipsychotic? I told my doctor that perhaps I needed something to push the pain/prayers down.

I took the communion, the ceremony I attended on Sundays, because I wanted to get the forgiveness I was promised, so I could die peacefully and go to Heaven—a place of rest, I was told.

I have mentioned to you that the last decade or so of my life has not at all given me a second to stop and breathe. My late teens and twenties, the ages that everyone is told are the greatest years you will ever experience, the years I will never get back . . . are gone. And I ask God why.

I ask God why, because I have realized that my life and my happiness have been stolen from me. I fought every voice that told me I was nothing. And commented on every move I made.

I took the pills as prescribed, ate the healthy food, and exercised.

Yet, I have nothing to show for my effort except side effects from pharmaceutical drugs and questions I asked my higher power that were never answered. Everything I thought I was born to do, to help others and change lives, has been taken from me. My depression and schizophrenia have killed a part of myself, my identity . . . the person I had hoped to become.

How am I to forgive myself?

After surviving in my body—a temple of God that is built in his image...

I survived, I say—

Isn't that enough?

No Contract for Safety

I told them I could not "contract for safety," you see.

In case you're not aware, a "contract for safety" is an agreement that patients can make with a doctor, therapist or other clinician, promising not to act on suicidal urges.

I don't remember being a danger to others, but I know what it's like to pray to my higher power—a God—my

God, to save me from myself, because today is not the day that I have control, nor is tomorrow, but—

Today is possibly the worst day of my life.

I hear loud, screaming voices cry out to me almost every day.

But it's different.

It's been more difficult, because they started to demand that I kill myself.

And it's terrifying when you cannot contract for safety because you cannot trust yourself.

Yes, I've been there.

Too over conscientiously aware of both my inner reality and outside world because it's too damn dangerous where I live.

Someone on my corner block once said to me that I have good insight into my illness.

And I felt like I was going to puke up chunks of their neurotypical privilege back on them.

For I am cursed with knowledge that I am at war with myself. Some people with my illness do not know they are mentally ill and unfortunately when I am going through a severe episode, I sometimes wish I didn't know I had this illness. I know this thinking is not appropriate; when I am suffering, however, my views can get cloudy.

But you see, I can't unscrew or remove the brain I was given. So, I am stuck with loud-ass neighbors, giving advice I don't want to hear, but I have to live with every single solitary day.

Like being in a cycle of verbal abuse.

You see, no one else can see or hear my Neighbor's Scream at me.

There is no curfew and I'm locked in a No Exit zone.

No way out.

I listen to the commands.

And as I said before, it's possibly the worst day of my life. Suicide looks so serene and serenity is what I seek.

Dedicated to My 22-Year-Old Self

I am a person who survived and learned to somehow deal with suicidal thoughts and auditory hallucinations. May I continue to always grow and learn new ways to reach my happiness. I wrote this poem to show people what it's like to live with schizophrenia and depression, but still have hope. If you can find hope in even one small thing, you can propel yourself forward.

After I wrote this, I felt a weight lift from my chest. I was able to feel like I accomplished something and put words to my pain. I helped calm myself down and temporarily relax, even with the suicide thoughts passing up and down.

I ended up getting help a few days later and seeking more treatment with my therapist. It helped greatly. I got my medication adjusted as well. And went to the hospital. Every hospital is different and every person has a unique experience at the hospital. Although they weren't great times, they helped me survive.

My chest has been hurting for a few days now, along with my headaches on and off. My neck and shoulders yell with pain as I walk. I'm getting more and more sick of this. I wake up today full of anxiety. This terrible feeling is swelling up within my entire body. I do not feel like I am living right now.

Instead, I feel as if I am being tortured by myself. It's as if a part of me is trying to choke the other half . . . trying to drain all the air out of me. Taking all my air, so that I can no longer breathe, hence I can no longer survive.

But I am still here fighting this battle within me. I'm still here!

I just get sick of doing this. I'm tired of episodes, depression, panic attacks, anxiety, insomnia. It's all too real. It's all too much a part of my being, which makes me angry and mad.

I don't want to deal with this any longer.

I think it's all too much.

Then that little voice, my saving grace, says, "Just keep going. Just hold on!"

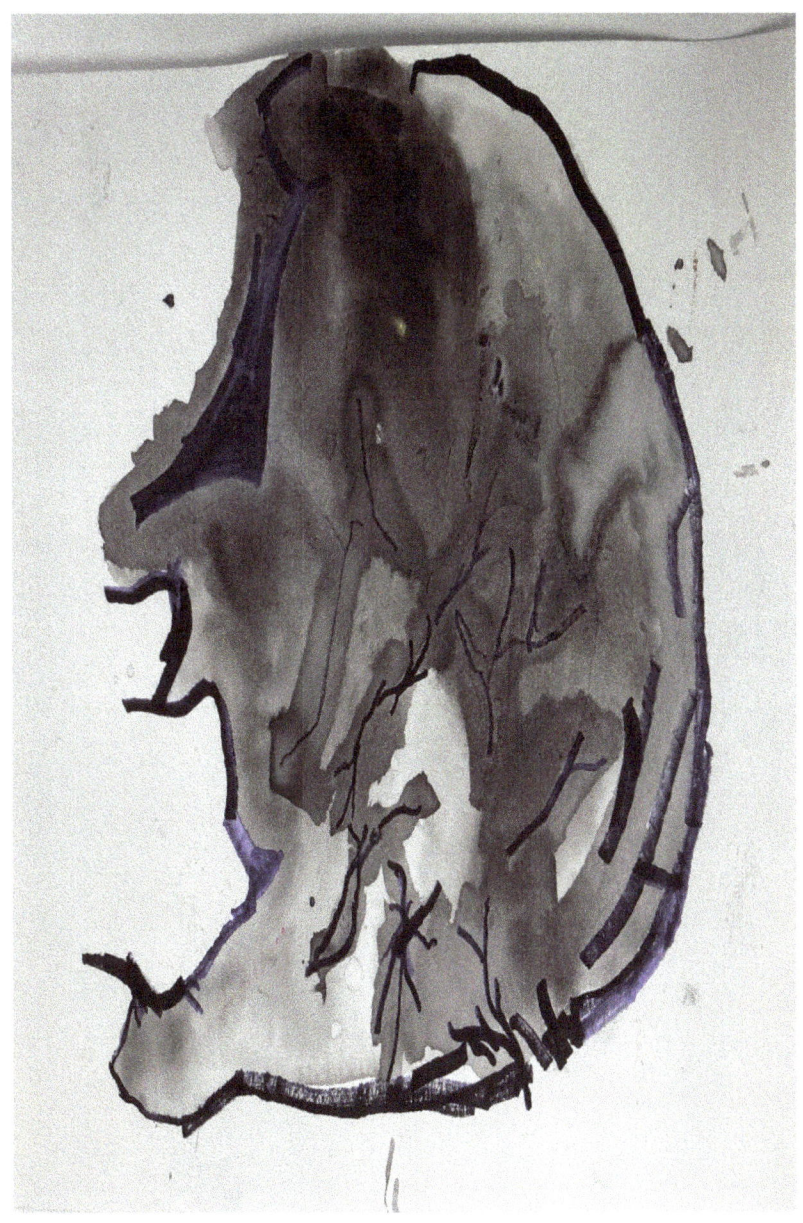

FACES PAINTING

Hope

I talked to Hope the other day.

She wasn't at all surprised where she found me...

I had my boxing gloves on—prepared for another fight, ready to go again all night,

To adjust my sails and follow a new path,

To trade my oars in and try a new form of transport.

I'll settle for no one—for nothing less—than my self-worth,

Which happens to be extremely high after I realized my mind was one of a kind, as is everyone on this planet we call home.

A place where we decide if our choices and our lives are destined or brimmed with uncertainties that no one knows really what will happen with time. I'll take the latter approach.

I'll go and say, "I'm going to live this day."

I'll live in the present moment—I live one day at a time. I'll fight and fall, I'll fall, I'll crawl, but at the end of the day, I'll get up and say, "Let me live for tomorrow, let me live for today."

I'll show you what I am made of; I'll give it another try.

I'll pick myself up from the ground and you see, I will fly.

Hope gives me wings. Today's the day—

I fly and rise to surprise, and show even the broken that Hope is close by.

I'll go higher and higher till I succeed—in proving to myself that I am worth more alive. I am worth more than a completed suicide.

Another person who is buried in the ground—leaving this earth too early for a temporary situation that may seem permanent, even chronic, in nature.

But nevertheless, it's pain that captures a person's soul—torments their being and prevents them from seeing.

Their future, their hope and sanity.

So, I beg you.

Let me say this again, I beg you—

To reconcile with the permanent decision you are about to make. Your life *is* worth living.

Hope said, again and again, "I'm here to fight for you.

"I've always been."

Keep Moving Forward

My mind may try to capture every weak spot I have and put it on display. But at the end of the day, there will always be tomorrow—as a blessing.

If we choose the path that has a road,

We can keep driving.

So, let's keep moving forward—keep going, keep breathing, and always remember that...

I fought today—so tomorrow I'd win. I'd win.

So tomorrow I'd win the lottery

a chance a day

that may bring me joy

so that my mental illnesses—won't scare me

so much as they have been

Doing all my life.

But instead

give me a chance to breathe and accept my health

the physical, too—in all its parts welded together

Are compacted into a vehicle that takes me to the places that make me

park my car and put on the radio and realize

For the first time—

That it may be just another Tuesday, but this Tuesday, I'm choosing

to be in the driver's seat.

Reckoning & Revelation

I had this thought I needed to share.

I'm writing this reckoning because I had a revelation. I am just realizing how remarkable my journey has been. How lucky I am.

And how thankful I need to be. I could have died multiple times by my own two hands—the same two instruments I use each day to pray these words onto paper. By many miracles, I'm alive and coherent,

cognitively apt—

so much more than just a damaged mess.

I am a fighter for all, an advocate for mental health and—

I'm never going to stop believing that everyone can make it out of the fire, too.

Because I know what it's like to be held hostage by one's mind. I know what it's like to be hospitalized against your will. I know how much hurt and struggle it takes to hear voices from all over berate you every single second of the day.

And not know if you will ever feel better again . . .

But trust in medication, trust in any higher power you desire—there will be a transformation. I found a way to live so loud, so beautiful that I'm no longer afraid of myself. Let's say that again: I used to be afraid that I'd end up killing myself—I no longer have that worry.

I'm instead happy and eager to plan for each day—each tomorrow, for everyday is a great way to celebrate that you and I are here together!!! So, let's celebrate.

We made it!!!

Together we are here.

Together we will share our journeys.

For this message is for you and my two hands.

The hands I used to use as a weapon against myself, but a means of healing now—a way of writing my story. Sharing my peace.

Because in the end, what I'm really doing is setting all my pain and suffering free.

A Healing Story

I need to tell you a story. Telling you this will help me heal. I moved in with my boyfriend at his sister's and brother in-law's house after living on my own in an apartment for about a year.

I didn't know, but my psychosis was getting much worse. I started to think certain people were following me and that those closest to me were critical of me to the point that they hated me. These people were my boyfriend's sister and her husband. I don't know why, but my schizophrenia decided that I was going to hear their voices in my head—and critique everything I did and scold me on tasks I performed in my living space. This became intolerable. I couldn't differentiate what was real and what wasn't. I was in the grip of severe mental illness and had no idea.

I also thought I heard the neighbors talking about me in negative ways and thought the government had hacked my phone and was trying to send me to prison. All of this was untrue. However, in my brain, I thought otherwise.

Due to my hallucinations—I put Sarah and Tom in turbulent stress quite a bit. Sarah and Tom being Jer's sister and brother-in-law. They didn't understand why I was being so dramatic and questioning. I had mentioned that I had mental illness when I first moved in, but they didn't know the severity. To this day, I am profoundly sorry about what I put these individuals through.

One day that changed our whole relationship was when they had to separate me from their home, when they realized that they had to set their own boundary. Accepting the fact that they could no longer live with me due to the nature of my psychosis—it was just too much for them to deal with—I had to move out of the house after they literally saved my life.

I was quite literally out of touch with reality. I was hearing voices. I thought I heard Sarah and Tom say they no longer liked me and actually hated me. I thought the police were going to be called and that I couldn't leave the house. I was confused and was convinced my phone was tracked and that I was being recorded and watched by the government. I heard the neighbors plotting to put a tracking device on me. Everything felt surreal.

During this time, Tom was actually checking on me and making sure I was OK—I didn't know that, though, because I was in psychosis. He ended up calling Jer because I was packing my things and calling my cousin who was a lawyer to figure out how to leave the house because I was afraid of the police. If he hadn't called Jer to come home from school early to talk to me, I don't know what would have happened to me because I was going to leave the house and drive while actively psychotic.

Tom saved my life that day. When Jer got home, he convinced me, along with Tom and Sarah later on, to go to a crisis center the next day and get help. I stayed there for four days and was then transferred to a hospital.

To this day, I feel horrible for being unaware of my actions towards Tom and Sarah, but I truly did not know what was going on in regards to my paranoia. It wasn't until a little over a year later that those memories resurfaced and I realized what exactly happened and I understood things through the psychosis lens. I now can see that I was wrong in thinking that Sarah and Tom hated me. That my brain was hijacked by my schizoaffective disorder. And today I can reality check more clearly and understand what is really happening in the world around me.

I am so happy to be able to see reality a bit more clearly. I still get confused and paranoid sometimes, but I am slightly able to differentiate it now, while using reality checking to decrease my anxiety and calm myself down. My therapy has helped me with this.

MANIC PAINTING

My Life, My Love

This is what you don't see—

My Life—as a mentally ill person

When the illness Starts to Manifest as something unlike the woman he first met.

When the man I love tells me he is scared to lose me. From my own mind.

The illness, he says, is looking a little rawer around the edges, more rough and jagged.

Not like you.

No, you are soft and beautiful. My illness, I interrupt, is hurting you as much as me. I'm sorry. I'm so sorry. I cry out to him. Pityingly, I fall into a ball of twine, twisted, up knotted—rooted—rooted together in a mess.

This brain disease is so harmful and stigmatized. My therapist once told me it would be better if I had cancer. Because at least with cancer, people have empathy.

Not with schizophrenia or its affective disorders. No, my schizoaffective disorder is just something people most likely run away from when they hear my diagnosis coming.

But I remember when we first met . . . I told you I had this illness . . .

But you were so, sooo different . . .

You were working,

and your medications were good.

You said you were stable.

I was stable for the time being.

But I told you, I told you this could happen.

I warned you.

I warned you of the monsters,

the voices—the pain—I told you.

I was a risk, you took a risk.

Now you lay next to your love.

But now I'm dying.

My brain is hijacked. It's trying to kill me. I can't function. The delusions are present. I think people are watching me, following me all around.

I can't tell you what is real, and what isn't. I'm terrified all the time. I try different medications and we go through difficult situations.

My love, I'm worried, so worried if you can or can't continue to handle my anxieties and eccentricities. Will you hold my hand and help me stand?

I'm unsteady, so unstable. I'm afraid to fall and I will do anything, even crawl.

If I have to.

Bethany, I'm taking you to the doctor, my love decides.

A crisis center awaits.

Next a locked ward opens its gates.

Severe mental illness is painfully showing itself. No longer looming in the back, but in the front of the room. My mental health degeneration is shown by the way I no longer have contact with reality.

I live within hallucinations and delusions of terror. But it's my turn to fight. I go to the hospital and try new medications. Do everything I can to get back to my old self.

I work hard, I go to therapy every week, and the psychiatrist every month.

This is what you do see . . .

My love, a man who stood by me and continues to stay by my side while I live with a form of schizophrenia.

Who understands my illness and what it is and how it works. My favorite person, the person who makes me the happiest.

A psychiatrist at a crisis center who helped me when I was at my lowest point of my life.

And me, a person living with a mental health condition, who is fighting to thrive each and every single day.

This is what you don't see when you prejudge and stigmatize a person with schizophrenia or any mental illness.

You miss out.

You miss out on understanding.

So, the person that I thought was gone was still here all along.

Mental illness never took her.

Hospitals

Hospitals are not always bad places to be—do not get me wrong. I know they are safe places where you can get the help you need. Trust me, I know there were times I needed a safe place to go when I was suicidal and the hospital provided me that safety. Not all hospitals are the same; there are good and bad ones. I was in one that was poorly staffed, so they couldn't manage all the patients. I have been in hospitals where things have been much calmer. It just depends on the place.

Never be afraid to get help, because even at the end of the day, the hospital where I had the worst time saved me from my severe psychosis and placed me on medication that helped me get through a part of my life I couldn't see myself moving through on my own.

This Book, My Saving Grace

This book has saved me. It has been my catharsis, my release and my saving grace. It has helped me with many of my obstacles and mental health challenges.

It sounds funny, but getting all the pain from my schizoaffective disorder out has made me a more conscious person. I still have my disability. I live with it every day, but I'm lighter now as a human. The grudge I carry because I have this illness is much smaller. And I'm thankful because of that.

Something else I've come to reconcile with is fear. I have learned much about how to live with fear, something that I struggle with each and every single day. Fear is a feeling. It's something everyone experiences, but because of my paranoia, I deal with it frequently. Learning and accepting that fear is a part of my life has been helpful in guiding me forward.

Life can be difficult at times when you live with mental illnesses, but I've learned to co-exist with them. One way I have done that is through therapy. Therapy taught me how to handle suicidal thoughts more peacefully—by accepting the thought for what it was and releasing it. It also enlightened me on how to exist with my traumas of schizoaffective disorder, because living with the hallucinations traumatized me in itself. For this, I had to learn that the auditory and visual hallucinations couldn't hurt me. And that they were in my head. Accepting the fact that the voices were in my head has been one of the hardest things I have ever had to do. But I'm coming along. By recognizing that the voices are within my own psyche, it helps me get a better understanding of my illness. This might help other people who are living with schizophrenia and struggling.

Schizophrenia also hinders your cognition and working memory. As a person progresses in age, the white and gray matter in a person with schizophrenia decreases, affecting many aspects of their life. Things like IQ can decrease—and deficits in thinking can happen. I personally have problems with memory and retaining information.

It affects my affect—facial expressions, tone of voice, gestures, posture and other physical expressions of my emotions. Sometimes my affect is off and it's hard to express the right emotion. Another area that schizophrenia takes over is motivation. I tend to have a hard time motivating myself to do simple tasks around the house, not out of laziness, but due to chemical levels in the brain not being high enough. Thus it takes me longer to complete various tasks.

All in all, schizophrenia takes different things from a person, but it doesn't take everything. I'm grateful for my life and everyone who's in it. Today I'm here to tell you I made it.

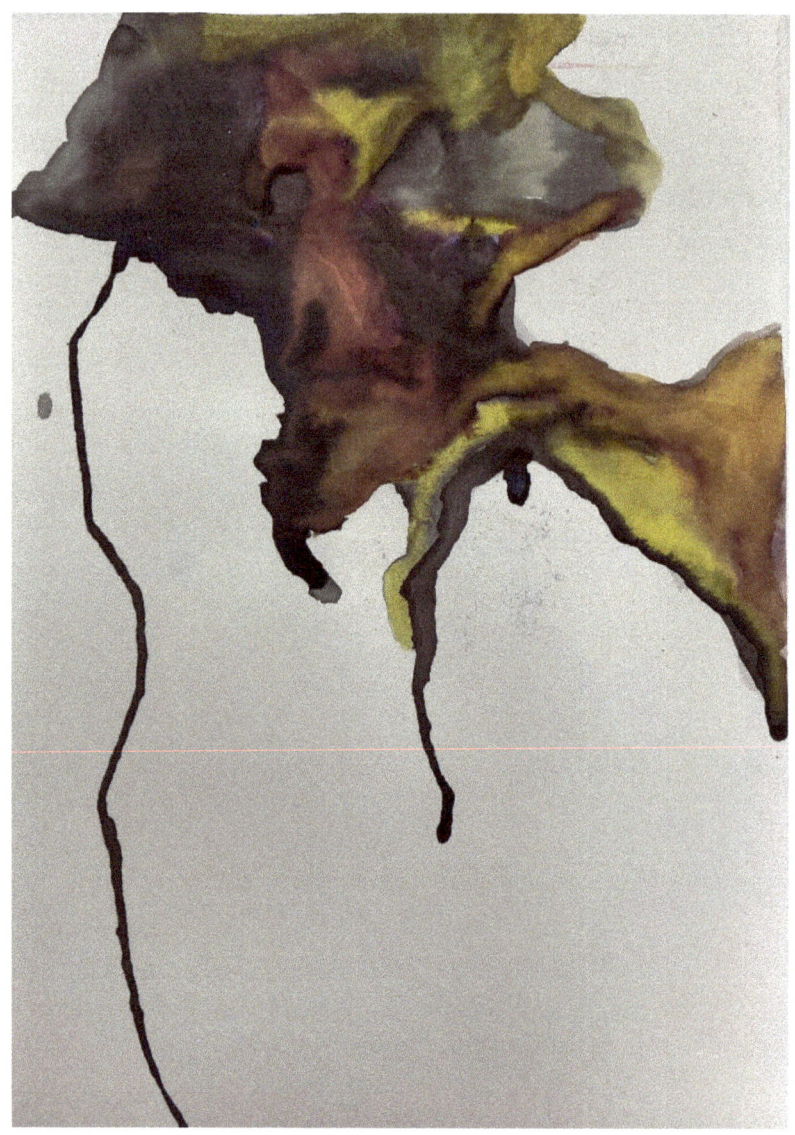

BRANCHES YELLING OUT TOWARDS THE SUN PAINTING

Survival in the Battlefield of a Neurodivergent Mind

I'm sick of puking up the word "survivor" like last night's spoiled leftovers. It's not a label I want. Resilient is another word for getting a beating and taking the abuse over and over. The vicious cycle at times you can't control. But I'm not here to give you definitions. I am here to tell you I reclaimed my life. I was beaten metaphorically and I'm still here to tell you my story. I knew at age 13 I was in for it, the first time depression swept me off my feet and kissed my lips, and mania whispered in my ear, "We've got you."

However, the illnesses I have didn't know how much I would fight back. How I would run and rip the brain diseases out of my body and mind. So, clarity would somehow come back.

You see, Peace is my holy temple. I occasionally reach it. I don't get cozy with the daisies every minute, hour or day, but sometimes I feel GREAT! And that in itself is a miracle. Happiness is sacred and I covet the feelings of joy. I mention this because I want to tell you I thought I would live in hell and never leave. I thought I would never be able to break free from my mental anguish, but I am able to for periods of time.

I am now 31 years old—living with schizoaffective disorder, bipolar disorder, PTSD, anxiety, depression and

ADD (Attention Deficit Disorder). But, despite this, I have many supports, including my "found family"—people who are not biological relatives, but who share unconditional love and encouragement with me. I love them dearly.

In my eyes, I am a success story. I tried to reach other dreams, but my life took a different path and that's OK because I have come to the conclusion that just being alive is the hardest and the greatest accomplishment I've ever made. Because being alive means I choose to continue living despite every painful second I've had to face.

But I realized that I have found joy in the little things and joy showed me that it can overturn hopelessness. By just finding the things that make me happy and people who make me smile. It was difficult, but I got the courage to make friends and try hobbies. I found the love of my life and get to share in his wonderful family.

At the end of this book, I just want to say, **do not be afraid of change**. Change can be good. Courage is hard at times, but when we free ourselves from the things that hold us back from getting healthy or better, it's easier to have good days.

So, push forward. Swing higher. Love harder. And fight. Fight for your life!

Because you deserve every beautiful thing this world has to offer.

ABOUT THE AUTHOR

Bethany Boik graduated from the University of Michigan-Dearborn with a degree in Behavioral Science from the interdisciplinary program in the College of Arts, Sciences and Letters. Bethany served two service-year terms in AmeriCorps and worked in the nonprofit field with at-risk youth and young adults in Detroit, Michigan.

In 2018, Bethany received the Youth United's Change Maker Award through the Detroit Wayne Mental Health Authority—for her work in developing youth voice. And in 2022, she received a Detroit Wayne Integrated Health Network Dreams Come True Award in the mini grant to assist the writing of her book, *Diary of a Schizophrenic*.

When she is not with her "love bug," the love of her life, or her family, she enjoys making multimedia art, painting and writing poetry. Bethany enjoys the company of her friends and loves listening to music, as it helps with her mental health. Currently she is listening to Machine Gun Kelly, Ryan Caraveo and NF.

You can contact Bethany by email at Bethanybwrites@gmail.com or find her on Facebook by searching for her name, Bethany Boik.

By reading *Diary of a Schizophrenic*, Bethany hopes you have gained a better understanding of mental illness and schizophrenia.

www.ingramcontent.com/pod-product-compliance
Lightning Source LLC
Chambersburg PA
CBHW051534120626
46551CB00012B/1216